Dogs

By Sally Cowan

Dogs can be pets.

My dog is big.

Nan's dog is not big.

It is a pup.

pup

Dogs can sit on rugs.

Dogs can get up and beg.

Dogs can run and run.

A dog can go on a big jog.

Dogs dig and dig.

Dogs can dig a big pit.

Dogs can dig in the mud.

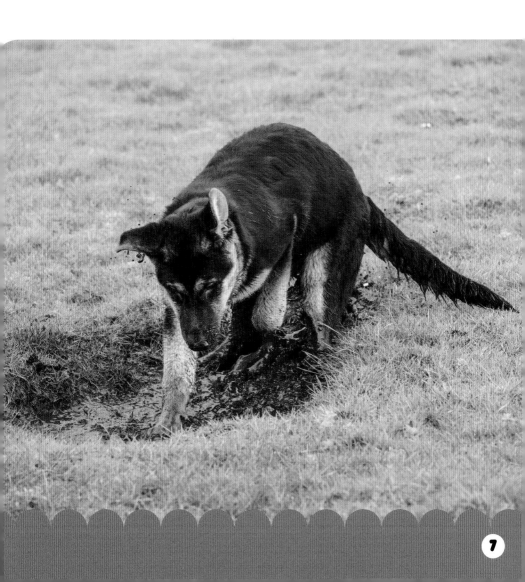

Dogs can go in a tub.

My dog gets in a big tub.

My dog gets a big hug!

CHECKING FOR MEANING

1. What size is the girl's dog? *(Literal)*

2. What sort of dog does Nan have? *(Literal)*

3. Why do you think the girl gives her dog a big hug? *(Inferential)*

EXTENDING VOCABULARY

pup	Find a word that has *up* at the end. Which other letters can go at the start of *–up* to make a new word?
rugs	How is the meaning of *rug* different to *rugs*? What other words in the text can be made to mean more than one by adding *s*?
beg	What does it mean to *beg*? Why do dogs beg? What might the boy give his dog when it begs?

MOVING BEYOND THE TEXT

1. Why do people like having dogs as pets?

2. What do you need to do to take good care of a dog?

3. What tricks can you teach a dog?

4. If you got a new dog or pup, what would you call it? Why?

SPEED SOUNDS

Dd	Jj	Oo	Gg	Uu

Cc	Bb	Rr	Ee	Ff	Hh	Nn

Mm	Ss	Aa	Pp	Ii	Tt

PRACTICE WORDS

dog

Dogs

big

not

pup

on

rugs

get

up

beg

dig

jog

run

and

hug

mud

gets

tub